Mind Over Matter

Beth Fiedler

Copyright © 2019 Beth Fiedler

ISBN: 978-0-9920937-8-5

All rights reserved. No part of this book may be reproduced or transmitted in any form or by any means, electronic or mechanical, including photocopying, recording, or by any information storage and retrieval system, without permission in writing from the copyright owner.

This book is presented solely for educational and entertainment purposes. The author and publisher are in no way liable for any misuse of the material. Although the author and publisher have made every effort to ensure that the information in this book was correct at press time, the author and publisher do not assume and hereby disclaim any liability to any party for any loss, damage, or disruption caused by errors or omissions, whether such errors or omissions result from negligence, accident, or any other cause. References are provided for informational purposes only and do not constitute endorsement of any websites or other sources. Readers should be aware that the websites listed in this book may change.

In certain cases the author has altered timelines and combined characters to improve the reading experience. Such alterations do not substantively impact the stories, which the author has endeavored to represent as accurately as she is able.

Printed in the United States of America

mindovermatter.bethfiedler.com

DEDICATION

This book is dedicated to my parents, my siblings Eva, Teresa and Leung, my husband Nelson and my best friend Terry, whose support and love continue to inspire me to live life to the fullest and share what I've learned.

ACKNOWLEDGMENTS

I thank my husband, Nelson, for sharing the journey of developing this animated book with me. I thank him for his continued patience and support when I lost myself in writing and publishing activities.

I thank my parents for a special childhood. I miss you every single day. I thank my siblings, Eva, Teresa and Leung, for the valuable memories we've created together.

I thank my NLP mentor, Linda Ferguson, for her guidance to expand my vision and become a better person plus many other devoted NLP practitioners who shared their stories with me.

I thank my personal and professional mentors for their guidance and insightful suggestions to help me look at things and experiences differently.

I thank my friends, associates, partners and customers, whom I am fortunate to know and work together, for their open, honest and supportive sharing of ideas and feedback across distance and space.

This book has been designed using resources from:

- Freepik.com
- Pixabay.com
- Vectortoons.com

INTRODUCTION

Thank you very much for this opportunity to share my stories with you!

What inspired me to create this animated book? It gave me an opportunity to review and refresh my life. I'm sharing my inner voice:

- What led me to where I am now
- What helped me to fulfil my dreams
- What guided me to continue my journey

This book was also inspired by NLP (Neuro-Linguistic-Programming). NLP is scientifically based and proves that our brain can reprogram itself to improve our lives by positively adjusting our experiences.

I want my book's takeaway to inspire the readers to relive their experiences, ie writing or drawing their stories on the space provided. By focusing on the benefits gained from their experience, Mind Over Matter helps to change their mindset in a positive way.

- Appreciate what happened from a different angle
- Make and explore more possibilities
- Persevere at achieving their dreams

You deserve to be happy, positive and lead a fulfilled life!

Having Fun

Small Please

Lost In Space

24/7 Enthusiast

Short Simple Sharing

Having Fun

Thanks Dad for the fun moments..

It was always a nice surprise to get a piggyback ride home

I've missed you since my 7th birthday

Love you!

Your fun moments

Only If I know

My dad was diagnosed with cancer

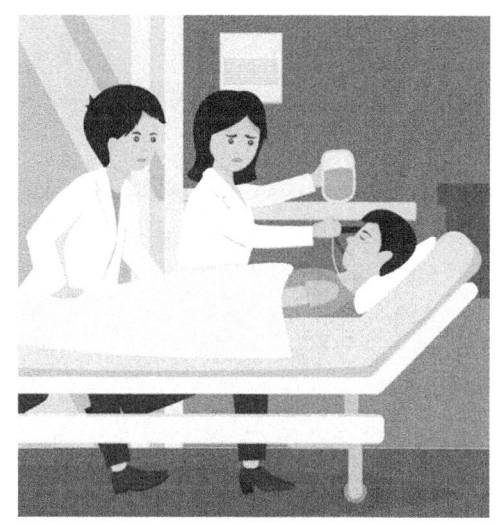

Didn't get a chance to visit and say goodbye

From a princess to a nobody overnight

3

Bonding Time

Oldest sister started working at 11

I'm the big sister of two young siblings

We were filled with joy after getting a loaf of bread. So little yet so much happiness!

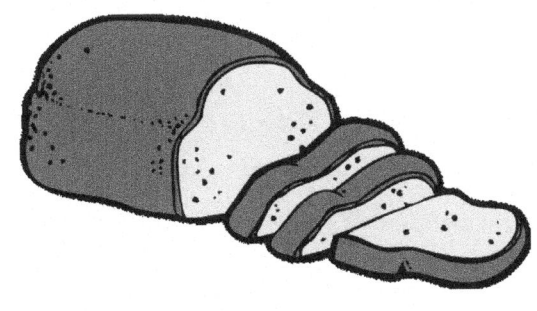

Food for thought

Small Please

Always a myth

Why the older kids will only get the small drumsticks

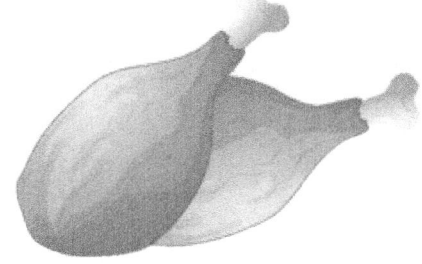

Until I'm old enough to realize it's our family tradition

Sorry mom!

First Battle

Curious to know why my mom would give me an empty bowl without rice?

I refused to overeat and chose to leave the rice untouched for weeks

Price to pay for my stubbornness = stomach pain

Thoughts

Spiral Loop

Will this nightmare ever stop?

It's been haunting me since dad passed away without saying goodbye

I ended up reading so that I could stay awake

How to fill a void

11

Loner

I seldom participated

because of peer pressure after losing my front teeth

Not speaking much and staying silent through most of my childhood

Your childhood

Lost In Space

Time isn't relevant when I was consumed in my own world

With minimal memories of childhood

Playing catchup with bits and pieces growing up

Your bits & pieces

15

Ugly Duckling

Grew up as the ugly duckling in the family

Wishful thinking that

I'll become a swan one day

19

Safety Blanket

Glasses for fashion or vision?

It gave me a false sense of identity

Glad that I'm no longer hanging on to them except ..

Your safety blanket

21

Knock Knock

I became unstoppable when looking for an overseas assignment

"What else" inspired me to try different things

I landed at the Beijing Airport because of CPR (**C**reativity-**P**ersistence-**R**esilience)

A new start with no family and friends

Good O Canada

Say YES to new adventures

CANADA

Let the fun begin

If I Never GO I'll Never KNOW

Your adventure

25

Back To School

Got up at 6:00 am and returned home after 9:00 pm

A bagel a day - my Breakfast-lunch-dinner combo meal

Best time of my life to accomplish my University dreams

Your best time

27

When a subway token is a luxury

Rewarding

See you next time

Enjoyed winter walks
-40 degree C

All worth It!

Your worth it

Bare Material

A flat carton box was my bed for months

Evening lab job made ends meet

Happy graduation with honors in less than two years

Your bottom line

31

happy

Feeling inspired and fortunate

What Kept Me Going

happy

I grew up with a big family of cats – over 10 at a time

Forever Love

Yellow overcame her physical challenge - a proud mom of 20+ fur babies

Yellow is my idol and BFF

Your BFF

35

happy

Hope

I daydreamt a lot

Having faith that things can only get better

Dream > Fear = Success

Hang in there

37

happy

24/7 Enthusiast

It's a blessing to stay energetic because I don't zzz much

Start everyday with a positive mindset

I'm determined to stay cheerful regardless of what lies ahead

Your enthusiasm

39

happy

Change Agent

Great to realize that we can't change others

I can change myself

That's how I uncover my hidden talents

Start with a small change

41

better

What If

Things to change if I have a second chance

better

Stay Whole

We didn't have a family photo with our dad .. only with mom

Your missing piece?

45

better

Mother's Love

My mom was a single parent of four small children

I missed our mother and daughter time

Our love is FOREVER

Love your mom

47

better

Sibling Love

When I was with my siblings, I felt whole

We shared special childhood memories

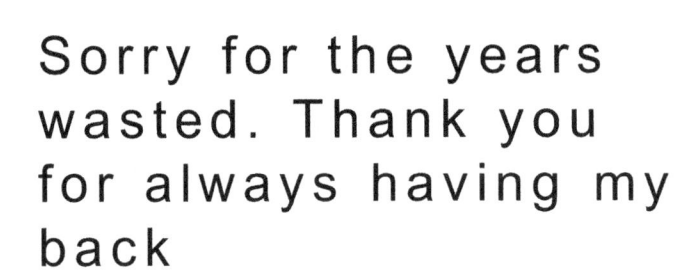

Sorry for the years wasted. Thank you for always having my back

Forever friends

49

better

Say It Loud

The more I held everything in

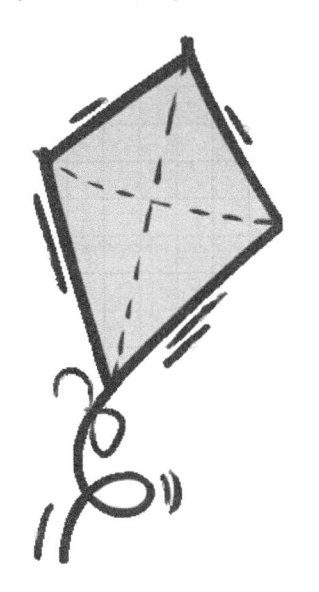

The more I shut down from the world

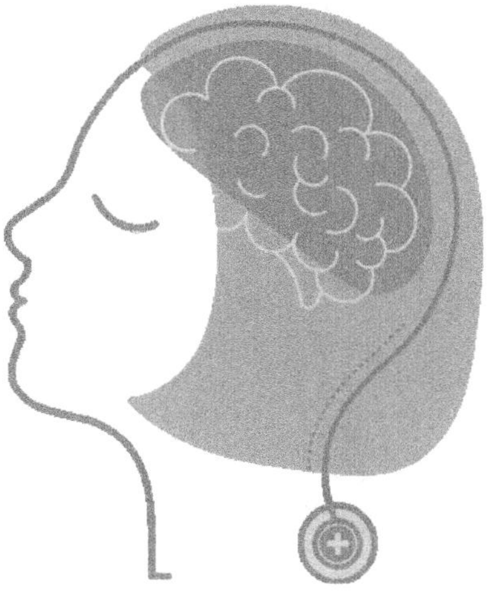

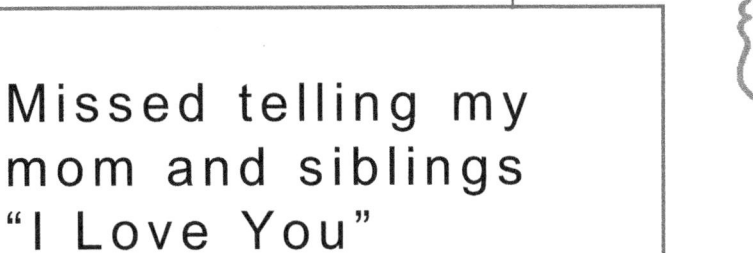

Missed telling my mom and siblings "I Love You"

Open up: ILY

51

better

Never Again

Going to watch a movie alone

Feeling extremely lonely

with all these people and so much laughter

Look for inner peace

53

better

Carrot Overdose

Interesting fact that I had a carrot muffin everyday for months

They were on sale for a dozen

Now I can't eat any carrot bakery goods

Interesting fact

55

better

Run Run Run

Hoping that a relationship would get better

when lots of tears were dropped and years were lost

Eventually I realized I can't change others and got out

Time to get out of ..

better

Giver Vs Receiver

I pride myself to be a giver until

I learned that receiving is equally important

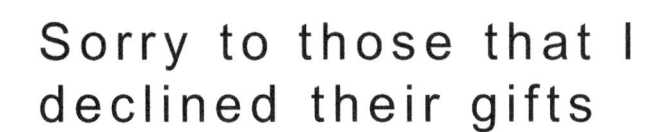

Sorry to those that I declined their gifts

Okay to receive

better

20/80

I used to put in 80% efforts to realize 20% results

Now I focus on 20% efforts to realize 80% results

Work life balance for inner peace and harmony

20/80 way to go

better

My Passion

I love training and sharing

Such a rewarding experience to see learners glow

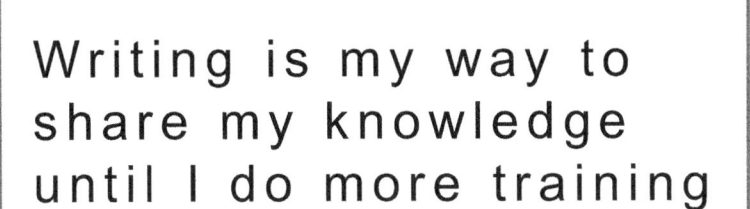

Writing is my way to share my knowledge until I do more training

Where your heart lies

best

Happy to share how I stay positive 100%

How Can I Do It

best

I used to be a perfectionist

Let Go

I was the one imposing unrealistic standards on myself

My current mindset is to do better every single day

Room to do better

67

best

Good Enough

Life is full of surprises

I always give my best shot to make things happen

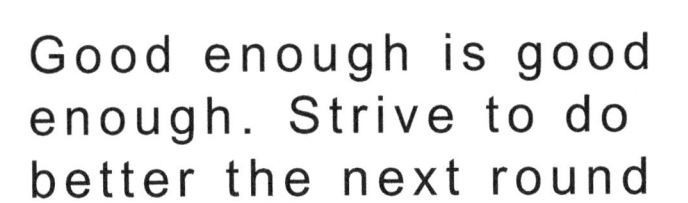

Good enough is good enough. Strive to do better the next round

Always a 2nd chance

69

best

I'm Different

There's only one ME

Unique and different in many aspects

Proud to be ME

Bravo to you

71

best

Okay To Say No

I said Yes to almost every request

It's actually okay to say No

Cool that I'm no longer a Yes lady

No is okay

73

best

When one door closes

Another Door Opens

Another door opens

Hey

I love this quote

"When one door closes, another opens; but we often look so long and so regretfully upon the closed door that we do not see the one which has opened for us."

Alexander Graham Bell

Look at the opened door

75

best

Understand ≠ Agree

It's a myth that most think

Understanding is the same as agreement

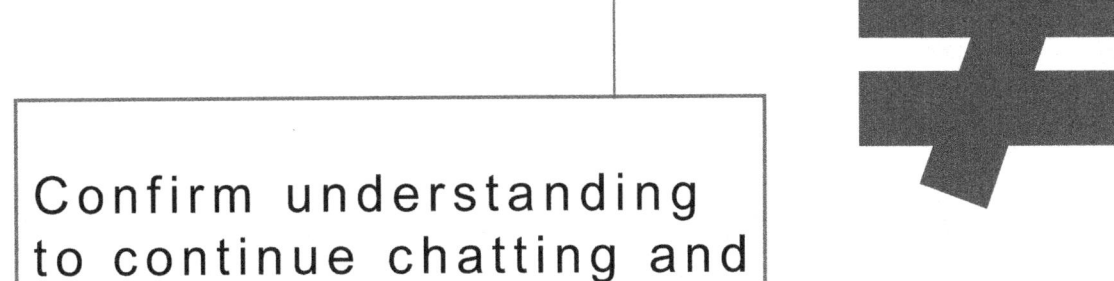

Confirm understanding to continue chatting and reach an agreement

Good to understand

best

Get Going

Whenever I feel stuck

OOPS

I become more creative and

physical moves help to shed more light

Go Go Go

79

best

No Response = Response

I felt restless waiting for a response

Until I realized no response was actually a response

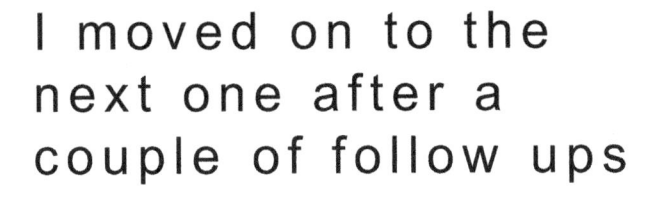

I moved on to the next one after a couple of follow ups

Accept a silent response

best

Forgiving & Forgetful

Wonder why I don't hold onto grudges

Being the one to forgive and forget

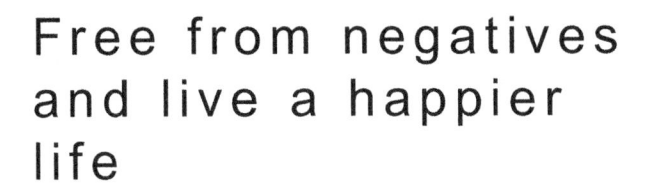

Free from negatives and live a happier life

Forgive please

83

Can Do attitude

What Else

What else I can try

Because I continue to explore

What else for you

85

best

Know What I Want

I give myself flexibility

To review and update what I want

I feel good to have an open mind

What do you want

best

More to share
See you next time

To be continued ..

BIOGRAPHY

Beth was born in Hong Kong. Her father was an electrical supply store owner who worked on personal and government projects. Her mother did the domestic work and planning for the store. They had three daughters and one son. Her father's unexpected death was the most traumatic event for the whole family as her mother was left with four young children from 2 to 9.

Beth emigrated to Toronto on her own and completed a Bachelor degree (honors) majored in Administration and Information Technology at Ryerson University. She pursued her passion and completed an Adult & Learning Development diploma with OISE Continuing & Professional Learning, University of Toronto.

Beth participated actively in the Toronto and Hong Kong Toastmasters communities. She was the first Area Governor/Distinguished Toastmaster in Hong Kong to win an Area Governor of the Year award in the Pan-Southeast Asia Pacific Region.

Beth has been a Reiki and NLP practitioner for over a decade. She refreshes these practices and completed her Advanced Reiki Master Teacher and NLP Practitioner/Master Practitioner certifications in 2019.

Beth appeared twice on the Dragons' Den reality show (Seasons VIII and IX). As her life goes on, she's devoting time to empower more souls to lead a happier life.

NLP Master Practitioner
Advanced Reiki Master Teacher
Coach, Trainer & Author

feeling

Get Creative

Opportunities to think differently

feeling

feeling

feeling

feeling

feeling

feeling

feeling

feeling

feeling

feeling

feeling

feeling

feeling

feeling

feeling

feeling

feeling

feeling

feeling

feeling

feeling

feeling

feeling

feeling

feeling

feeling

Made in the USA
Monee, IL
08 September 2019